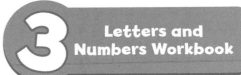

3 Letters and Numbers Workbook

T0134214

○ **Trace.**

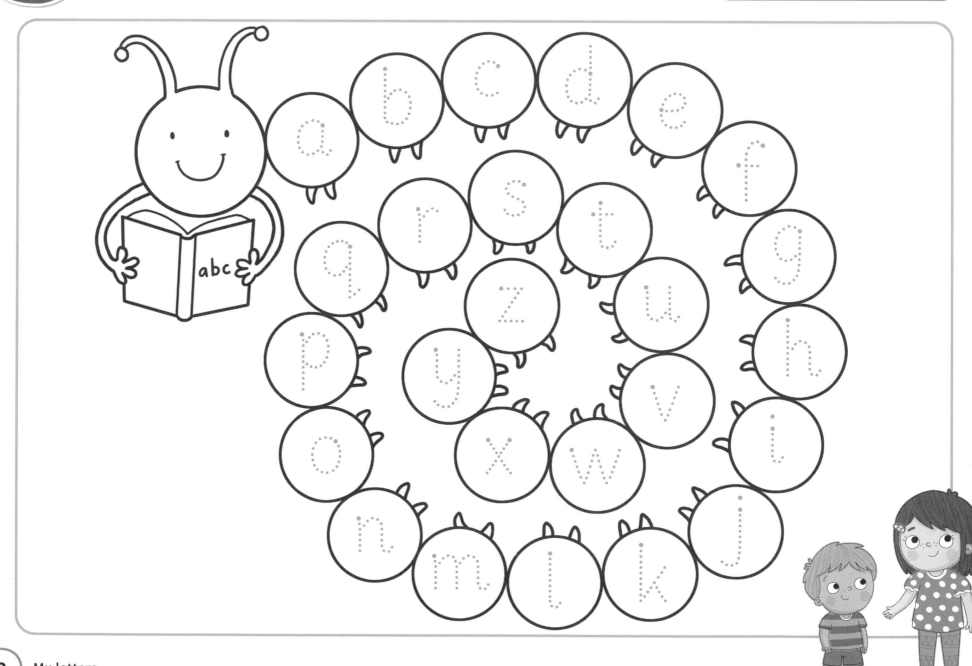

 # Match. Color.

Review the alphabet. Then the children look at the letters and draw a line to match them with the corresponding pictures. Finally, they color the pictures freely.

a	c	e	g	j	m

⭕ Circle. ✏️ Color.

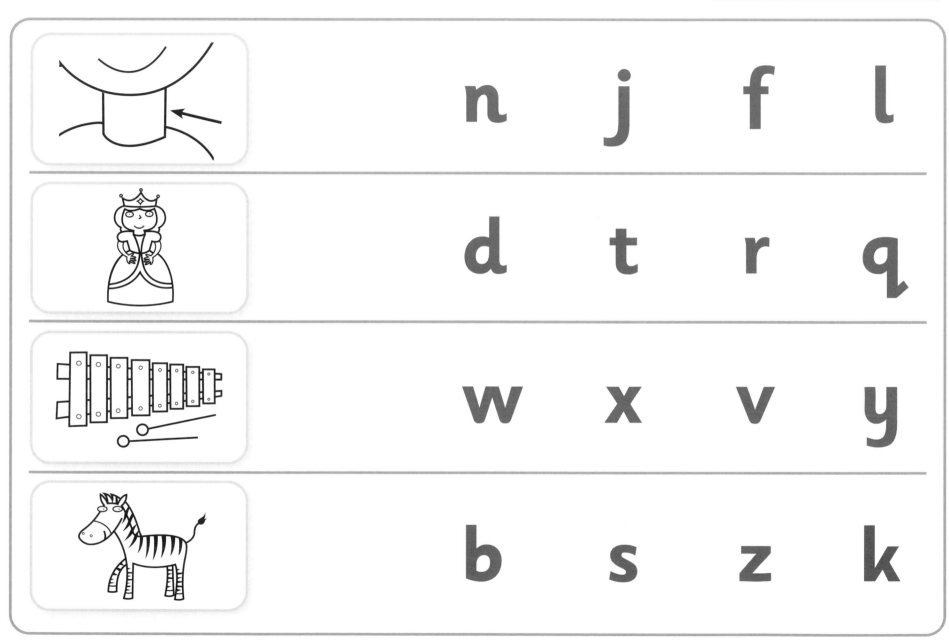

n   j   f   l

d   t   r   q

w   x   v   y

b   s   z   k

✋ Count. ⭕ Circle. ✏️ Color.

Review the numbers from 1 to 5. Then the children count the objects in each box and circle the corresponding number. Finally, they color the objects and numbers freely.

2 5   4 3   2 1

1 4   4 5   5 3

◯ Trace. ✋ Count. ✏️ Color.

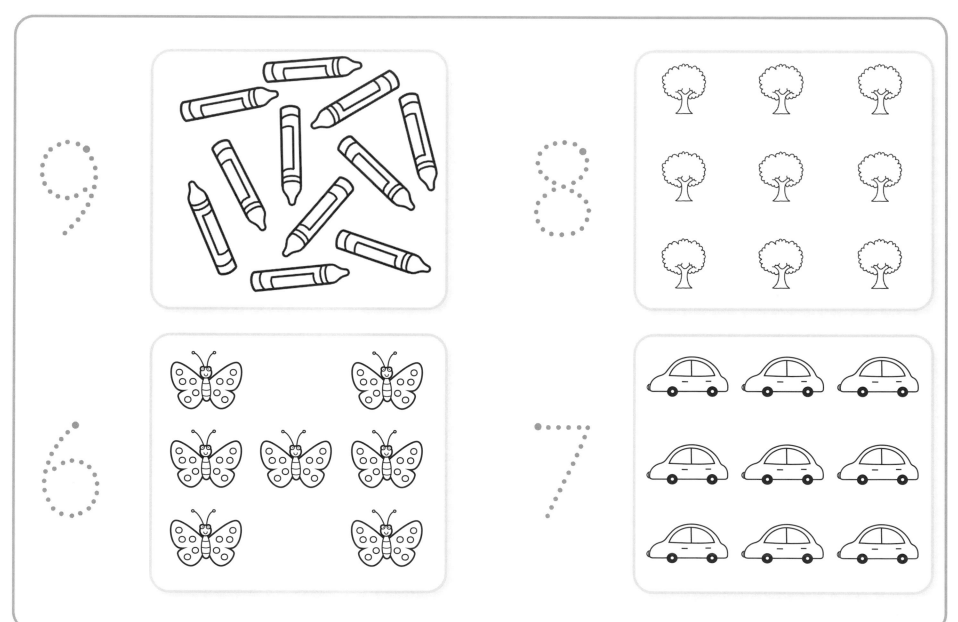

✏ Write. ✏ Color.

Review the numbers from 1 to 10. Then the children look at the first series of numbers and write the missing number. Repeat the procedure for the remaining series. Finally, they color the pictures freely.

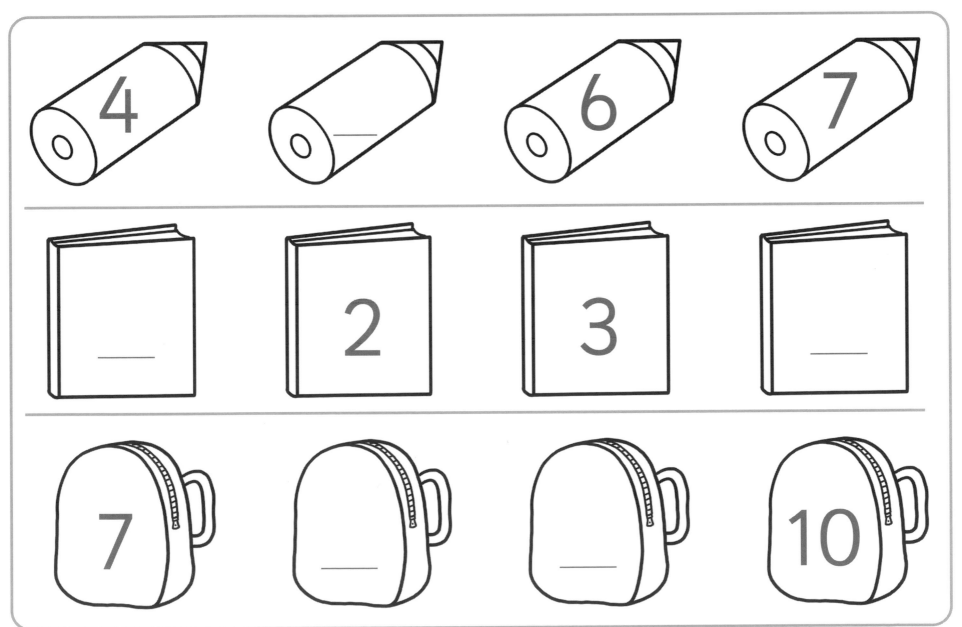

◌ **Trace.** ✏ **Color.**

The children identify the daily activities.
Then they trace the words with colored pencils.
Finally, the children color the pictures freely.

have breakfast

brush my teeth

wake up

get dressed

⬭ Trace. ✏ Color.

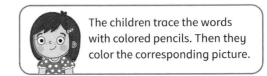
The children trace the words with colored pencils. Then they color the corresponding picture.

I wash my face.

I brush my hair.

I have breakfast.

 Trace. Match. Color.

The children trace the words with colored pencils. Then they match the sentences with the corresponding pictures. Finally, the children color the pictures freely.

I wake up every day.

I get dressed every day.

I wash my face every day.

 **Follow.** 🖊 **Draw.** 🖍 **Color.**

 Review the numbers from 1 to 20. Then the children connect the dots. Ask *What is it? A house!* Finally, they color the house freely.

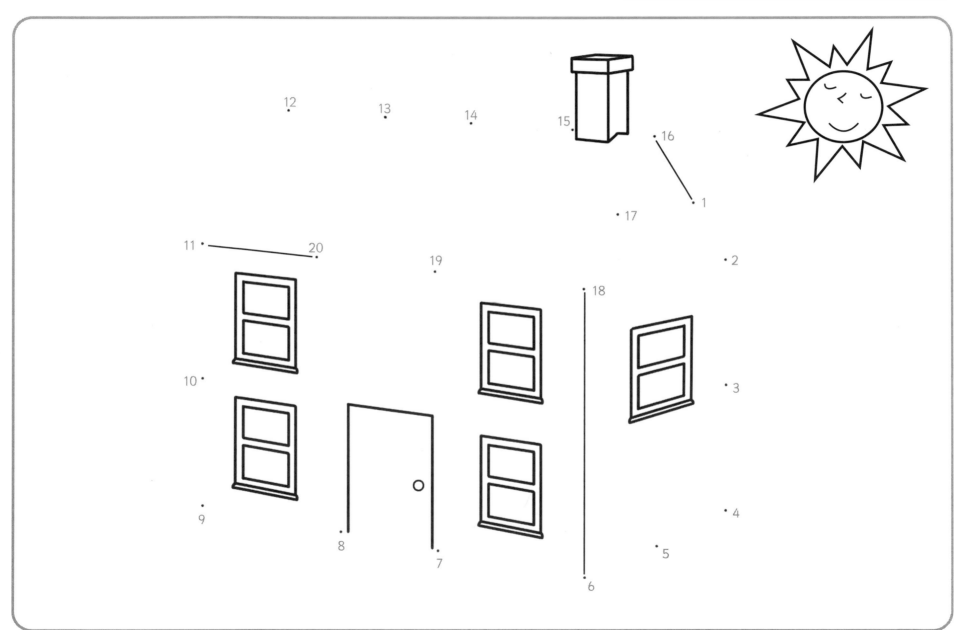

✋ Count. 📓 Match. ✏️ Color.

 Review the numbers from 1 to 20. Then the children count the dots on each bed. Next, they draw lines to match the dots on the beds with the corresponding numbers. Finally, the children color the pictures freely.

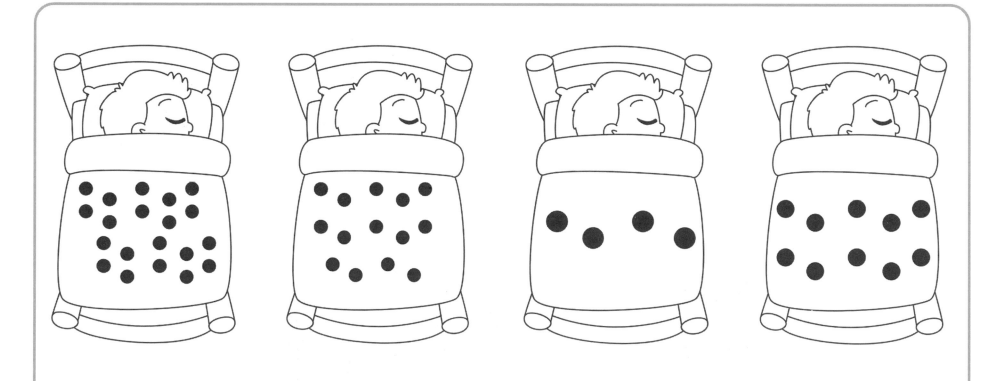

10   4   14   20

 Count. Write.

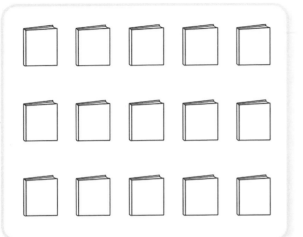

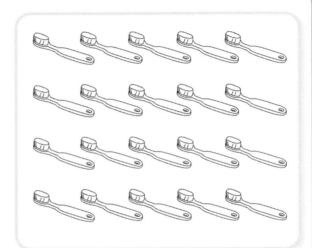

_____

_____

_____

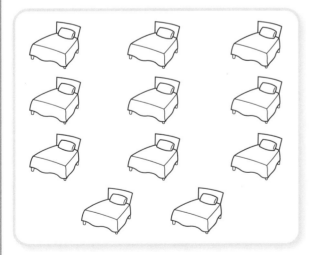

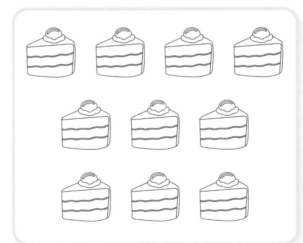

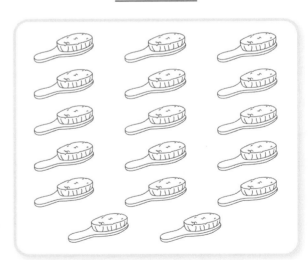

_____

_____

_____

My numbers (13)

📙 **Match.** ⭕ **Trace.** ✏️ **Color.**

The children trace over each path with a red crayon. Then they trace the corresponding words with colored pencils. Finally, the children color the pictures.

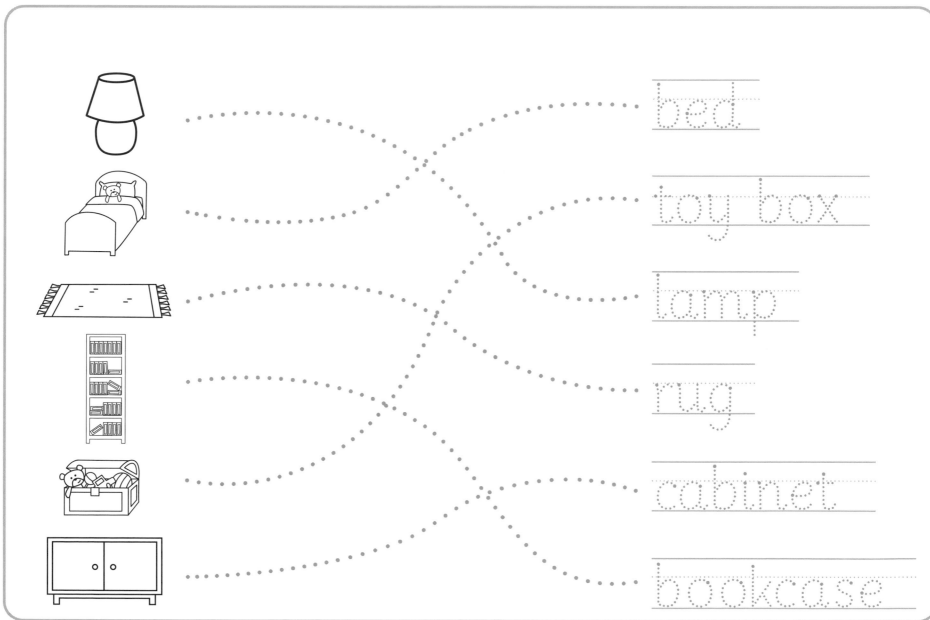

bed

toy box

lamp

rug

cabinet

bookcase

○ Trace.  Match. ✏ Color.

 The children trace the words with colored pencils. Then they draw lines to match the sentences with the corresponding pictures. Finally, the children color the pictures freely.

It's next to the cabinet.

It's on the bed.

It's in the toy box.

○ **Trace.** ○ **Circle.**

The children trace the words with colored pencils. Then they circle the correct pictures.

It's under the rug.

It's on the bookcase.

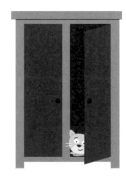 

It's next to the lamp.

 **Count.** **Color.**

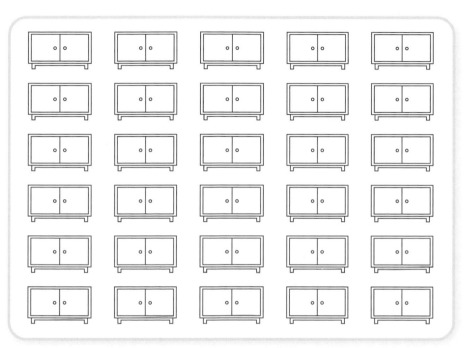

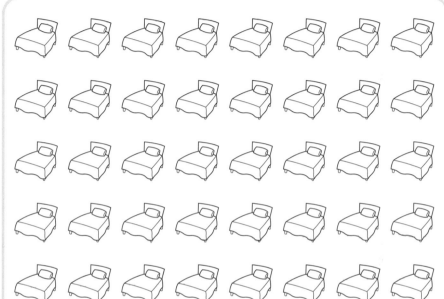

30

40

 **Count.** ○ **Circle.**

 The children count the objects in each box. Then they circle the corresponding number.

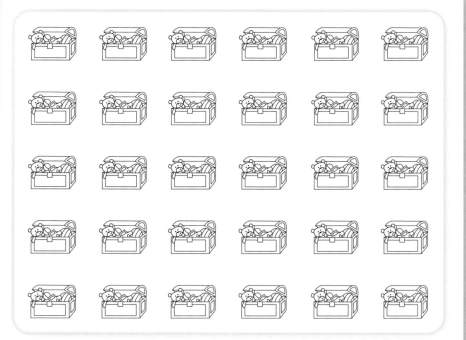

30 40

30 40

 **Count.** **Draw.**

The children count the objects in each box. Then they draw five more of each object to show the correct number.

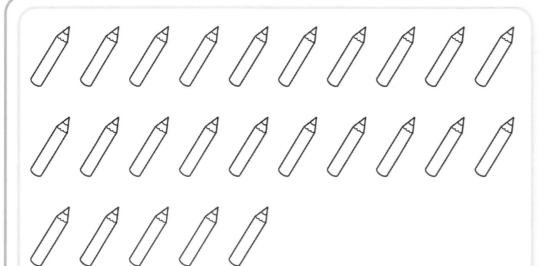 **= 30**

 **= 40**

Unit 4

✏️ **Write.** 🖍️ **Color.**

The children write the words in the boxes under the correct sport. Then they color the pictures freely.

badminton	baseball	basketball
field hockey	soccer	tennis

○ **Circle.** ✏ **Write.**

 The children circle the corresponding word above each picture. Then they copy the words onto the lines.

badminton **basketball**

He's playing   .

baseball **tennis**

She's playing   .

baseball **soccer**

They're playing   .

⭕ Circle. ✏️ Write.

field hockey
baseball

They're playing _____.

basketball
soccer

They're playing _____.

badminton
tennis

They're playing _____.

 **Count.** **Match.** **Color.**

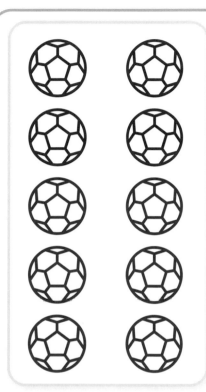  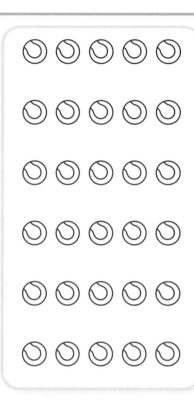 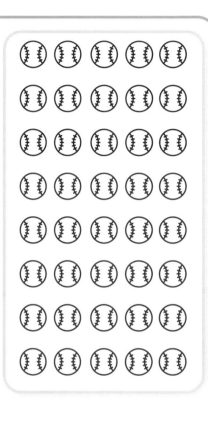

30 40 10 20

 **Count.** ◯ **Trace.**

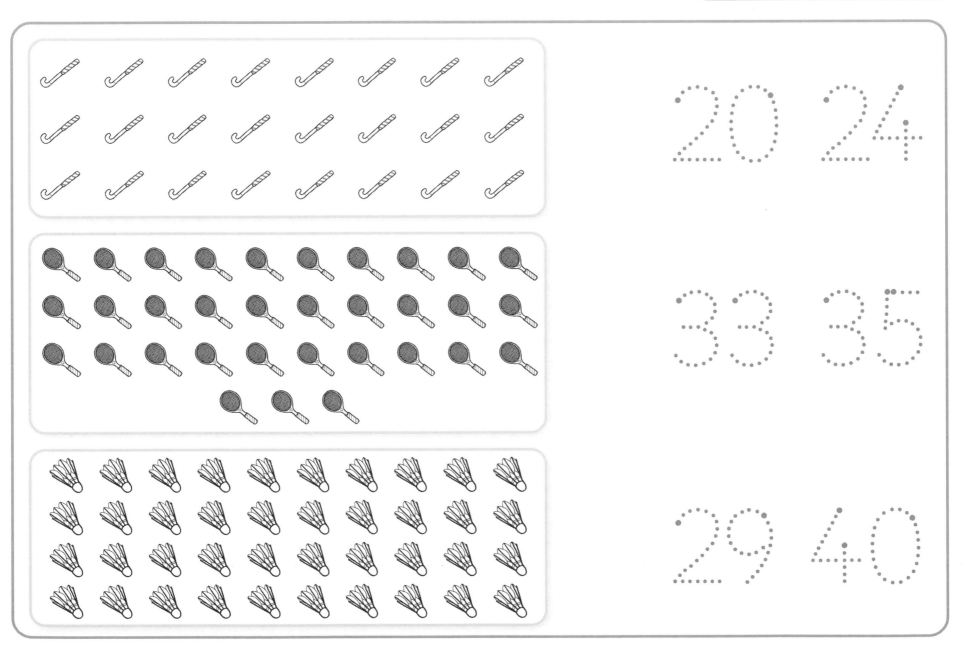

20   24

33   35

29   40

 **Write.** 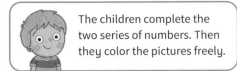 **Color.**

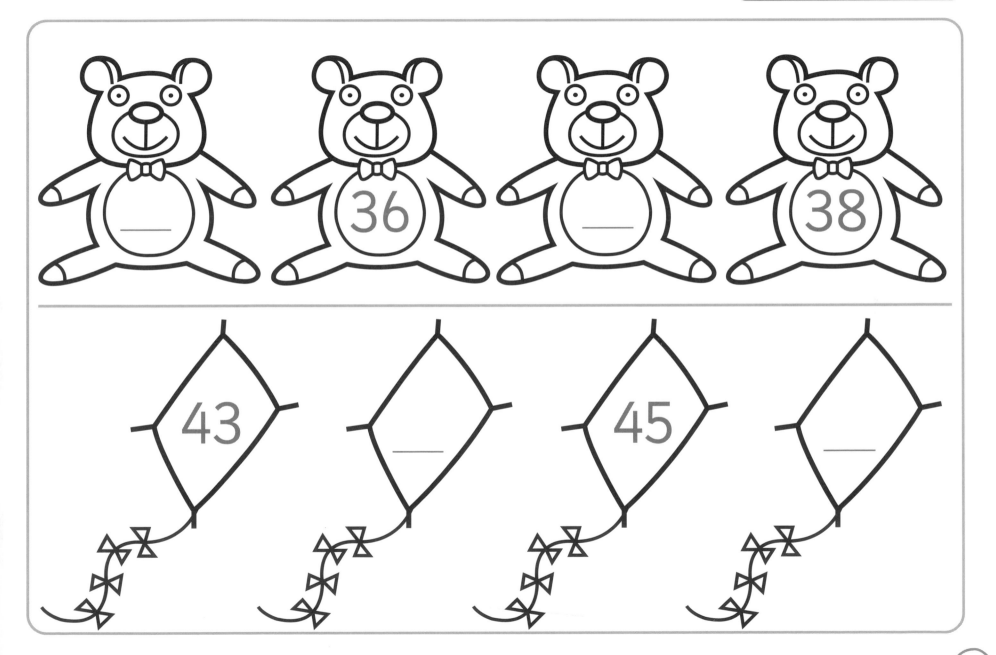

Unit 5

✏️ **Write.** 🖍️ **Color.**

reading books   listening to music

watching TV

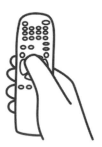

⭕ Trace. ✏️ Write. 🖍️ Color.

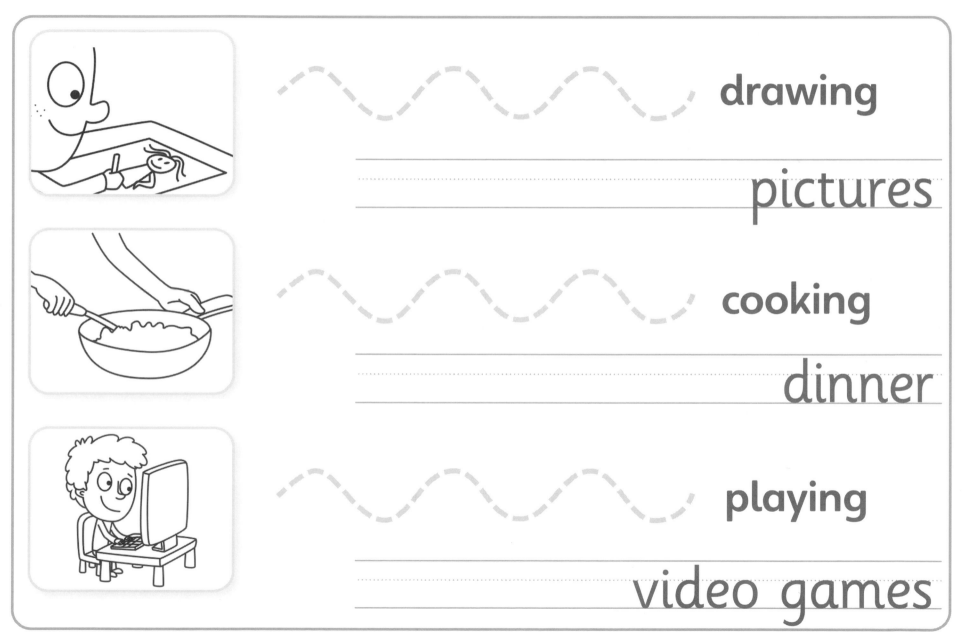

drawing

pictures

cooking

dinner

playing

video games

✏️ Write. 🖍️ Color.

reading books

We like _____ .

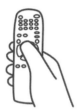

watching TV

I like _____ .

drawing pictures

I like _____ .

 **Count.** ◯ **Trace.** ✏️ **Color.**

10

20

30

40

50

 Count. ✏️ Color.

 Present the number 60. Then the children count the bubbles in the bathtubs in sets of tens. Finally, they color the pictures freely.

60

 Count. ◯ Circle.

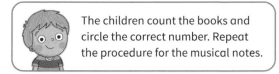 The children count the books and circle the correct number. Repeat the procedure for the musical notes.

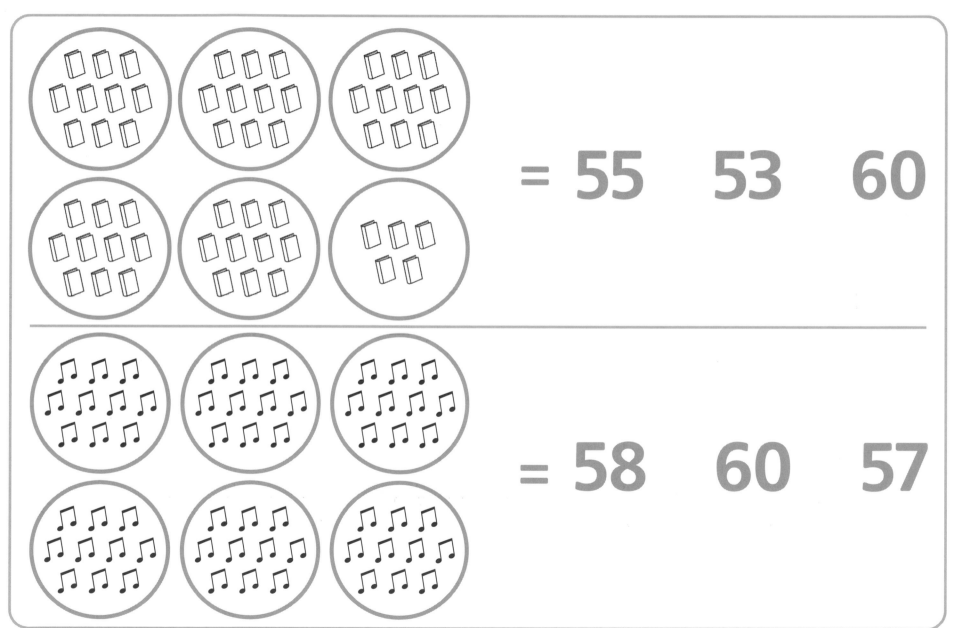

= 55   53   60

= 58   60   57

⬭ Trace. ✔ Write a check.

The children trace the words and write a check next to the correct pictures.

chocolate

☐   ☐

grapes

☐   ☐

pineapple

☐   ☐

○ **Trace.** ○ **Circle.**

Would you like some sweets?

Would you like some chips?

Would you like some cake?

⭕ Trace. 📘 Match.

The children trace the sentences. Then the children draw lines to match the sentences to the correct pictures.

I'd like some cake.

I'd like some chocolate.

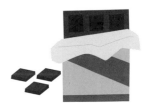

I'd like some grapes.

✋ Count. ✏️ Write. ✏️ Color.

 The children count the food items in each box. Then they write the corresponding number next to each picture. Finally, the children color the pictures freely.

How many?

 _____

 _____

 _____

 **Write.** **Color.**

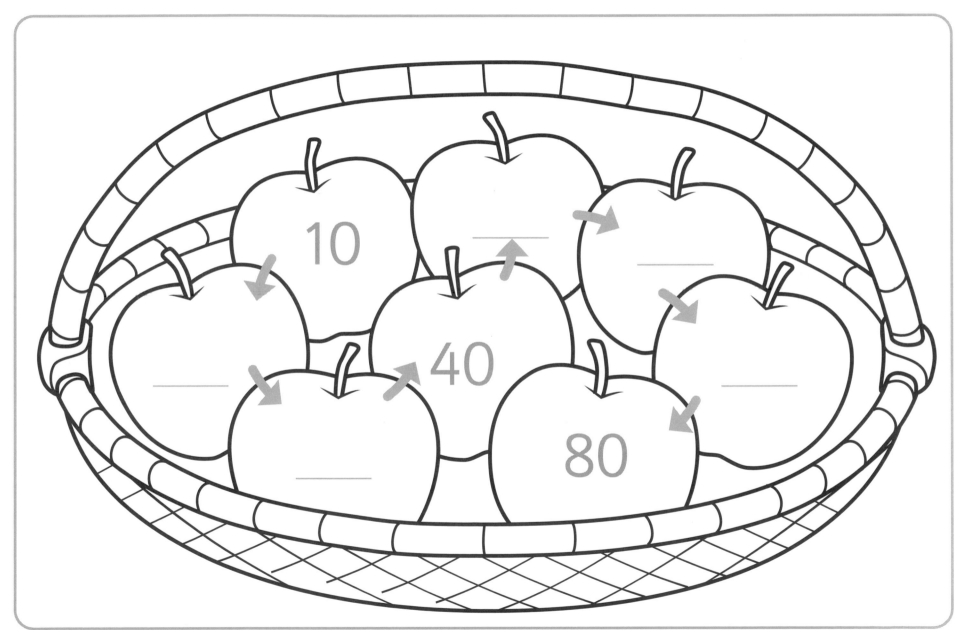

Trace. **Draw.** **Color.**

The children trace the sentences. Then they draw and color the animals' missing body parts. Finally, the children color the animals freely.

There's a monkey.

There's a tiger.

There's a snake.

⭕ Trace. ✋ Count. ⭕ Circle.

The children trace the sentences with colored pencils. Then they circle the correct number of elephants, hippos and crocodiles.

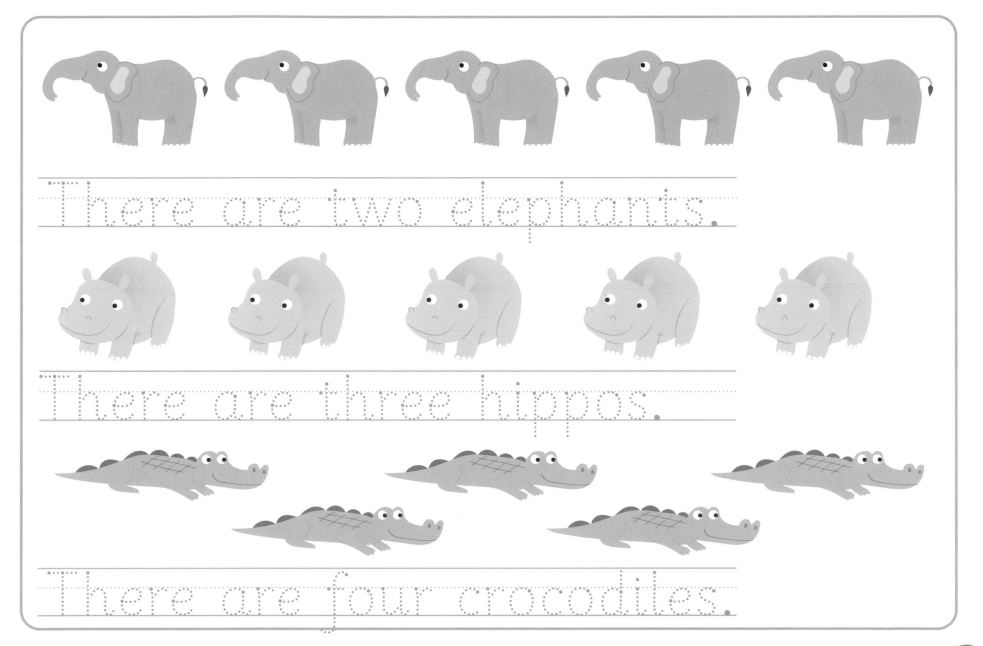

There are two elephants.

There are three hippos.

There are four crocodiles.

◯ Trace. ✏️ Draw.

The children trace the sentences. Then they illustrate each sentence.

There's a snake.

There are two elephants.

There are three hippos.

 **Count.** / **Paint.**

 Present the number 70. Next, the children count the sheep in tens. Finally, the children paint the number 70. Alternatively, they can color the number with crayons.

My numbers 41

 **Count.**  **Color.**

80

Follow. Draw. Color.

Review the numbers from 1 to 80. Then the children connect the dots and form a rabbit. Finally, they color the rabbit freely.

 **Read.** ✏ **Write.** ✏ **Color.**

Plants need rain.

Plants

Plants need soil.

Plants need sun.

 **Read.** ◯ **Circle.** ✏ **Write.**

 **What beautiful flowers!**

What .... !

 **What an old hat!**

.... !

 **Read.** ✔ **Write a check.** ✎ **Write.**

Plants need rain.

Plants need sun.

Plants   .

What an ugly garden!

What a beautiful garden!

!

✋ Count. ✏️ Color.

 Present the number 90. Then the children count the trees in sets of ten. Finally, they color the number 90.

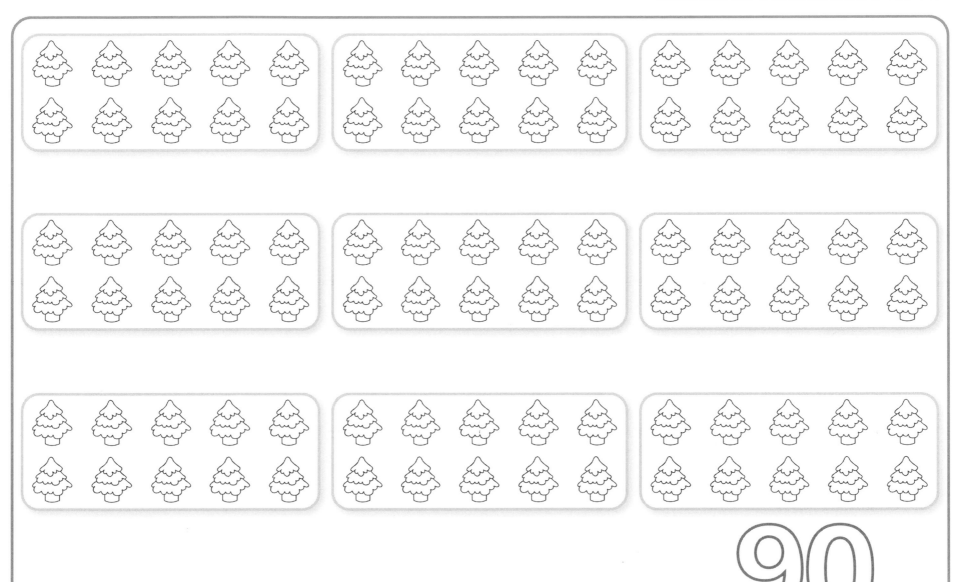

90

 Count. ✏️ Color.

 Present the number 100. The children count the suns in sets of ten. Then they color the number 100 freely.

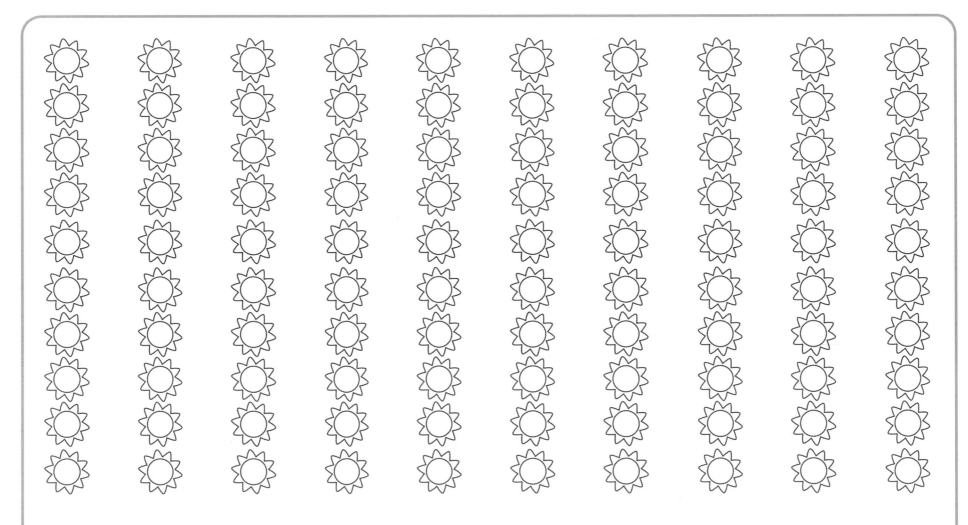

100

✋ Count. ○ Circle.

Review the numbers from 80 to 100. Then the children count the seeds and circle the corresponding number. Repeat the procedure for the leaves.

How many?

85   **90**   **93**

90   **95**   **100**

📖 **Read.** ✏️ **Write.** 🖍️ **Color.**

The children complete the sentence with the words *to the supermarket*. Repeat the procedure for the remaining items. Finally, they color the pictures freely.

We're going to the playground.

supermarket   **restaurant**   **hospital**

We're going   .

📖 Read. ✏️ Write. ✏️ Color.

 The children read the sentence. Then they copy the words *works in a ...* and complete the sentence with the word *store*. Repeat the procedure for the remaining sentences. Finally, the children color the pictures freely.

 A teacher works in a school.

  **sales clerk**  **store**

A sales clerk _____.

 **doctor**  **hospital**

_____

 waiter  **restaurant**

_____

✏ Write. 🖊 Color.

The children connect the words to form sentences. Then they copy the sentences onto the lines. Finally, the children color the pictures freely.

I'm going → to → the playground.

I'm going _____.

We're going → to → the store.

_____

We're going → to → the restaurant.

_____

 Review the numbers from 10 to 100. Then the children write the missing numbers on the path with colored pencils. Finally, they color the picture freely.

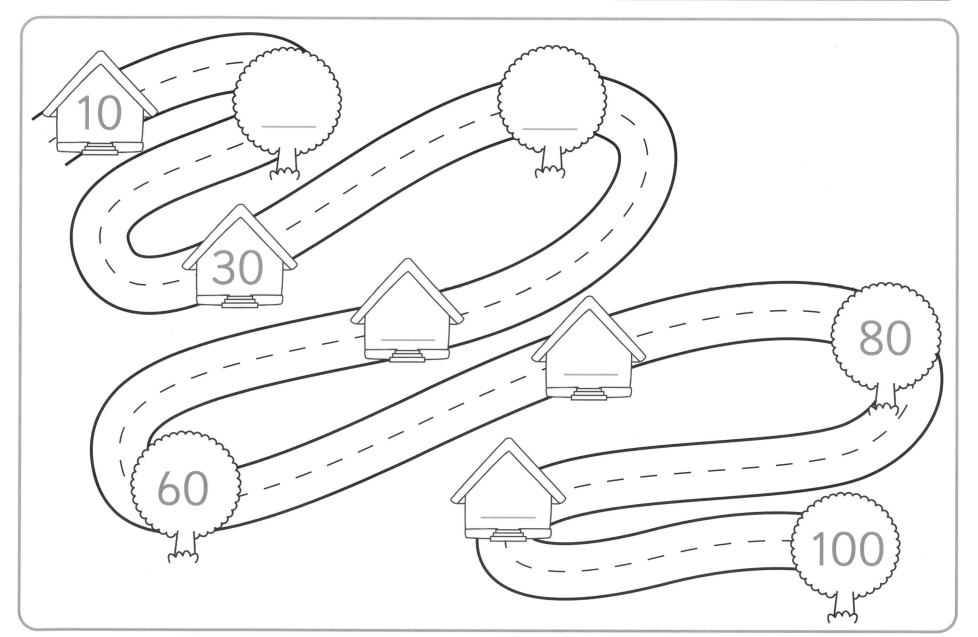

My numbers 53

 **Draw.** **Color.**

Review the numbers from 10 to 100. Then the children identify the number 10, draw a line from the number 10 to the number 20, and so on, using a colored pencil. Finally, they color the numbers freely.

10   70

20   80

60

30

90

50

40   100

My numbers

✋ Count. ✖ Cross out.

Say *There are twenty-two bikes. We only need twenty bikes. Cross out the extra bikes.* The children cross out two bikes. Repeat the procedure for the remaining objects.

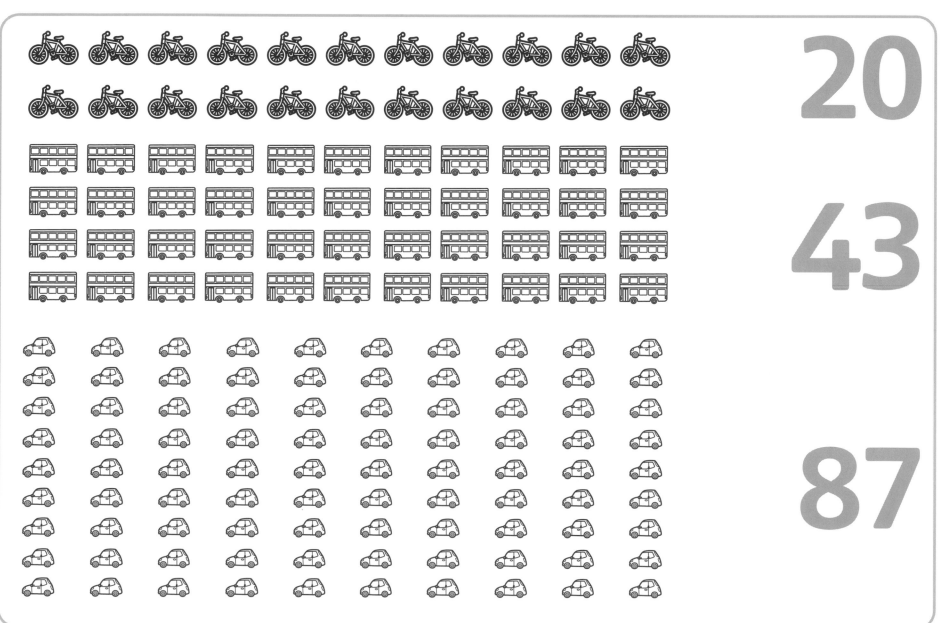

20

43

87

Thanks and acknowledgements

The publishers and authors would like to thank the following contributors:

Page makeup by Blooberry Design and QBS Learning.
Cover concept by Blooberry Design. Front cover photography by
NYS444/iStock/Getty Images

Illustrations by Louise Gardner, Marek Jagucki, Sue King (Plum Pudding), and
Bernice Lum. Icons (color, count, draw, look, match, say, trace, tick, write) by
https://thenounproject.com/icon.